D0481147

Holiday Gift-Giving
Recipes

Muriel Miura

MUTUAL PUBLISHING

ISBN-10: 1-56647-753-0
ISBN-13: 978-1-56647-753-6
Library of Congress Catalog Card Number: 2005931014

Photographs by Ray Wong
Design by Emily R. Lee

First Printing, October 2005
Second Printing, November 2007

Mutual Publishing, LLC
1215 Center Street, Suite 210
Honolulu, Hawai'i 96816
Ph: 808-732-1709 / Fax: 808-734-4094
Email: info@mutualpublishing.com
www.mutualpublishing.com

Printed in Korea

Table of Contents

Foreword

The greatest gift is a gift of yourself—your time, your talent, your consideration of the recipient's taste and needs.

This is why a taste of home—whether baked in a cake or bottled in a jar—is always greeted as a gift from the heart.

From Raspberry Vinegar to Pineapple Bell Pepper Relish, Liliko'i Vinaigrette to Papaya Curry Marinade, Spicy Kaki Mochi to 'Ono Lemon Coconut Bars, Muriel Miura's *Holiday Gift-Giving Recipes* offers a wealth of suggestions that will be well-appreciated by friends and relations both here and away.

Introduction

Holiday Gift-Giving Recipes offers you some of my favorite recipes for gift-giving. I loved putting together this special collection of recipes, especially with the holidays in mind. It was so much fun working on this book as many of the recipes evoked fond memories of past holidays. In addition, research focused on tips to make the results in baking and cooking so much better and more consistent.

Bottles filled with flavored butters, vinegars and oils, or jars filled with seasoned salts, rubs, and spices then topped with colorful fabrics and bows will undoubtedly brighten any gift basket. Island flavored jams and marmalades of guava, papaya-pineapple or poha gives any toast, cracker, or scone that exotic taste.

During the holiday season, relatives and friends drop in to extend holiday greetings. Serve your guests Cranberry Nut Bread, Pumpkin Bread, or Macadamia and Cranberry Scones with whipped honey-butter or sweetened cream—delicious! With advance notice, you can even bake and serve the elegant Guava Chiffon Pie, Pumpkin Cheesecake, or scrumptious Rum Cake.

The cookie recipes will offer you "Aha!" moments in baking. All the recipes are brief and the directions simple. The cookies are all deliciously addicting but my favorite is the 'Ono Lemon Coconut Bars. Also, the Christmas Cookies are easy to decorate, and most cookies can be packaged attractively with little effort. Because cookies are probably the most popular gifts, following are some of the tips that I'd like to share with you:

- ❖ To keep logs of refrigerator cookie dough from flattening on one side as they chill, rest them in a trough made from a halved paper towel core.
- ❖ To keep cookies from spreading too much in the oven, be sure to use butter that's just soft enough to cream with the sugar, but not so warm that it melts the moment it gets in the oven; chilling dough also ensures cookies will keep their shape.
- ❖ Instead of a knife, use a bench scraper to cut bar cookies into neat pieces.
- ❖ Cookies usually bake most evenly on flat cookie sheets.
- ❖ To chill cookie dough faster, divide it into smaller portions and shape it into disks.
- ❖ If you don't have a food processor, you can easily make crumbs for a cookie crust by putting the cookies in a zip-lock bag and crushing them with a rolling pin.

You'll have fun making Gifts-in-a-Jar. It is a wonderful project to get the children involved and they can also help in making the confections such as Chocolate and Macadamia Truffles, Coconut Candy, and Fudge.

Salad dressings, pickles, and preserves are always appreciated by the receivers, as are sauces like Maui Barbecue Sauce, Papaya Curry Marinade, Zesty Cranberry Sauce, and Delicious Chocolate Sauce. If little gifts are what you need, make some of the snacks and munchies in this book. Who can resist Caramelized Macadamia Nuts, Cinnamon-Sugar Spiced Macadamias, Homemade Arare, and more? They are all simply delicious snacking foods that can be made in a jiffy—well, more or less—and certain to please everyone's palate.

You'll find many opportunities to make use of this collection of time proven recipes planned to bring year-round cooking and giving pleasure. Plus, we've included some ideas on ways to decorate and wrap your homemade items.

Baking or cooking items for gifts is a lot more fun when you can do it at your convenience, not the night before you need them. Use your freezer! Many weeks before the height of the season, wrap the cookies in small batches and place them in larger containers so that you can quickly pull out a few cookies as needed. Besides, they stay crisp and fresh in the freezer and thaw out in minutes.

Whichever recipe you choose to make for your friends or loved ones, they will be delighted to receive it. Gifts from the kitchen are always cherished because of all the love and thought that goes into their preparation and wrapping.

In the true spirit of the holidays, sincerest best wishes to you and your loved ones for a happy and safe holiday season.

Muriel Miura, CFCS

CAKES,
COOKIES,
AND BREADS

Guava Chiffon Pie

Makes two 9 x 5-inch loaves

9-inch baked pie shell
1 envelope unflavored gelatin
1/4 cup water
4 eggs, separated
1/4 cup lemon juice
3 tablespoons sugar
1 (6-ounce) can frozen guava juice, thawed
1/2 teaspoon cream of tartar
1/2 cup sugar
2 cups whipped cream or nondairy whipped topping

Soften gelatin in water; set aside. Beat egg yolks, beat in lemon juice and 2 tablespoons sugar; cook over low heat, stirring constantly until mixture is thickened. Stir in softened gelatin and remove from heat; cool; stir in guava juice and chill until mixture begins to thicken.

Beat egg whites together with cream of tartar until soft peaks form; gradually add remaining sugar, beating until stiff. Fold in thickened guava mixture; pour into pie shell and chill until firm, about 3 hours. Serve with whipped cream or topping.

TIPS FOR FREEZING PIES

Use cookie crumbs to make a shortcut crust; add a creamy or chiffon filling for an impressive but easy dessert. If you don't have a food processor to make cookie crumbs, put the cookies in a zip-top bag and crush with a rolling pin. Lay a piece of plastic wrap over the crumbs as you spread them in your pie pan so they won't stick to your hands.

Rum Cake

Makes 10 servings

1 cup chopped nuts
1 (18-1/2-ounce) package yellow cake mix
1 (3-3/4-ounce) package instant vanilla pudding and pie filling
4 eggs
3/4 cup water
1/2 cup salad oil
1 cup dark rum
1/2 cup butter or margarine
1 cup sugar

Grease and flour 10-inch tube pan. Sprinkle nuts on bottom of the pan. Combine cake mix, pudding, eggs, 1/2 cup of the water, oil, and 1/2 cup of the rum; mix well. Pour batter over nuts in pan. Bake at 325 degrees Fahrenheit for 1 hour. Cool and invert onto serving plate. Using a fork, prick top of cake. To make glaze, melt butter in saucepan. Stir in remaining 1/4 cup water and the sugar; boil 5 minutes, stirring constantly. Stir in remaining 1/2 cup rum. Drizzle glaze over top of cake.

TIPS

Never fill the pan more than two-thirds of the way with batter. For full-size loaf or bundt pans, leave over an inch of space at the top. For mini pans, divide the batter evenly so that the cakes bake at the same pace.

Pumpkin Crunch with Cream Cheese Frosting

Makes 24 servings

1 (29-ounce) can solid pack pumpkin
1 (12-ounce) can evaporated milk
1 cup sugar
3 eggs, slightly beaten
1/4 teaspoon ground cinnamon
1 box yellow pudding cake mix
1 cup walnuts, chopped
1 cup butter, melted

Mix pumpkin, evaporated milk, sugar, eggs, and cinnamon together. Pour into a 9 x 13-inch pan lined with waxed paper. Sprinkle dry cake mix over the pumpkin mixture. Pat nuts on cake mix. Spoon melted butter evenly over all. Bake at 350 degrees Fahrenheit for 50 to 60 minutes. Invert onto a tray and peel off the waxed paper. Cool. Frost with cream cheese frosting (see below).

Cream Cheese Frosting
1 (8-ounce) package cream cheese at room temperature
1/2 cup sifted powdered sugar
3/4 cup Cool Whip

Beat together the cream cheese and powdered sugar. Fold in the Cool Whip. Spread evenly over the cake and cut into squares.

Pumpkin Cheesecake

Makes 12 servings

Crust:
1-1/2 cups graham cookie crumbs
1/2 cup nuts, finely chopped
1/4 cup brown sugar, packed
1/3 cup melted butter

Filling:
1 pound cream cheese
8 ounces mascarpone cheese
1 cup sugar
1 cup pumpkin
3 eggs
2 teaspoons cinnamon
1 teaspoon ground ginger

For the crust: Combine graham crumbs, nuts, and brown sugar in a bowl; mix to blend. Add melted butter and toss to moisten. Press mixture into the bottom of a 10-inch springform pan.

For the filling: In a large bowl, beat the cream cheese, mascarpone, and sugar together until smooth, scraping sides often. Add pumpkin and beat until smooth. Add eggs, one at a time, beating well after each addition. Add the cinnamon and ginger; beat until smooth.

Pour batter into the prepared crust and place springform pan on a baking sheet. Bake at 300 degrees Fahrenheit for 50 to 60 minutes, or until cheesecake begins to pull away from the sides of the pan and is light brown. Cool to room temperature. Cover and chill overnight before serving. To serve, top with sweetened whipped cream.

Chocolate Shortbread

Makes 54 cookies

Shortbread Crust:
2 cups all-purpose flour
1/2 cup sugar
1/4 teaspoon salt
1 cup butter, softened

Chocolate Macadamia Filling:
2 cups semisweet chocolate chips
1/4 cup butter
6 eggs, slightly beaten
1 cup sugar
2/3 cup light corn syrup
2 teaspoons vanilla extract
2 cups finely chopped nuts (macadamia, pecan, or walnut)

Preheat oven to 375 degrees Fahrenheit.

For the shortbread crust: In a large bowl, combine flour, sugar, and salt. Cut butter into the flour until texture is mealy. Press mixture evenly into the bottom of a 9 x 13-inch pan. Bake at 375 degrees Fahrenheit for about 15 minutes, or until lightly golden. Set aside.

For the filling: Melt chocolate and butter together in the top of a double boiler over simmering water. Whisk until smooth. Set aside.

In a large bowl, beat eggs and sugar together until well blended. Stir in chocolate mixture, corn syrup, and vanilla. Stir in nuts. Pour mixture over the shortbread crust. Bake at 375 degrees Fahrenheit for an additional 25 to 30 minutes, or until filling has set. Remove from oven and cool completely. Cut into 2-inch squares.

TIPS

Big or small, cakes do well at 350 degrees Fahrenheit. Keep the oven temperature the same for any size pan.

Adjust your timing to fit the pan. Full-size bundt pans take 40 to 50 minutes. Standard loaves take 45 to 50 minutes. Mini bundt cakes and mini loaves take anywhere from 20 to 35 minutes.

Know the signs of doneness. Cakes are done when a wooden skewer inserted in the center comes out clean or with only a few moist crumbs clinging to it. For mini cakes, use a toothpick instead of a skewer.

Check thrift shops for china plates, baskets, or silver trays, which make nice keepsakes after the cake is gone.

To give specialty pans as gifts, bake the cake in the pan, wash the pan as the cake cools, and return the cake to the pan before wrapping.

Make a gift basket to go along with the cake. Include the recipe and any special ingredients like macadamia nuts, gourmet chocolate, or vanilla beans from Kona.

Christmas Cookies

Makes about two dozen cookies

2 cups all-purpose flour
1/2 teaspoon salt
1 cup butter (unsalted preferred), softened
3/4 cup sugar
1 large egg
1-1/4 teaspoons vanilla extract

Combine flour and salt in a medium bowl. Set aside. With electric mixer, beat the butter and sugar until light and fluffy. Beat in egg and vanilla. Beat in flour mixture just until combined. Remove dough from bowl, gather into two balls or disks; wrap each in plastic and chill until firm, about 2 to 3 hours.

To bake, line cookie sheets with parchment; set aside. Flour work surface and the rolling pin. Roll one dough disk 1/4 inch thick. Cut out into desired shapes (star, Christmas tree, Santa, snowflake); decorate with sprinkles as desired before baking (if using). Reroll the dough scraps to make more cookies. Bake at 325 degrees Fahrenheit for 13 to 16 minutes or until edges turn golden brown. Let cool completely before transferring or decorating with Royal Icing as desired. Repeat with second disk of dough.

continued on next page

Royal Icing

4-1/4 cups confectioners' sugar, sifted
3 large egg whites
1/2 teaspoon cream of tartar

Combine all ingredients in large bowl; mix on low speed of mixer until well blended. Increase to medium speed and beat until icing holds thick, soft peaks, about 4 to 6 minutes. Test icing for outline consistency by piping small amount through a decorative tip. If icing tends to curl back or is difficult to pipe out, add a few drops of water or if it is runny, add more confectioners' sugar, a tablespoon at a time, beating on low speed to blend. Tint as desired with food coloring; keep all colors separated.

TIPS

Always chill the dough until firm

Roll dough out to an even thickness so that the cookies will bake in the same amount of time.

Lightly flour sharp edge of cookie cutters to prevent dough shapes from sticking to cutters

Decorated cookies should be dried on racks for at least six hours.

Oops—if you've made a mistake and want to redo a decoration, wipe off the area with a slightly damp paper towel. If the icing has dried, simply scrape off with a small knife.

Cookies decorated with Royal Icing are best stored in airtight containers at a cool room temperature. Freezing can cause the icing to separate from the cookies.

Almond Cookies

Makes 4 dozen cookies

2 cups flour
1 cup sugar
1/2 teaspoon baking powder
1/2 teaspoon salt
2/3 cup shortening
1 cup chopped almonds
1 beaten egg
2 teaspoons almond extract
Red food coloring

Sift flour, sugar, baking powder, and salt together. Cut in shortening until mixture is like cornmeal. Add chopped almonds. Mix egg and almond extract. Add to flour mixture. Mix well and knead gently 30 minutes. Form into balls the size of quarters. Place on ungreased cookie sheet. Dip chopstick in red food color and make an indentation in the center of each cookie. Bake at 350 degrees Fahrenheit for 15 minutes.

FREEZING COOKIE DOUGH

Form refrigerator cookie dough into rolls. Wrap in plastic wrap or freezer paper; press out excess air, seal, label, and freeze. Thaw dough in refrigerator about 1 hour or until dough slices easily. Pack other types of cookie dough in freezer containers. Seal, label, and freeze. Thaw until dough handles easily.

Energy Bars

Makes 36 bars

2-1/2 cups crisp rice cereal
1 cup quick oats
3/4 cup toasted sesame seeds
1 (10-ounce) package marshmallows
1/2 cup peanut butter
1/4 cup butter
1/4 cup peanuts
1/4 cup raisins

Grease a 13 x 9 x 2-inch pan and set aside. In a saucepan, combine rice cereal, oats, and sesame seeds; toast over medium heat a few minutes. In a large saucepan, combine marshmallows, peanut butter, and butter; melt over low heat. Stir in cereal mixture, peanuts, and raisins. Press firmly into prepared pan. Cool; cut into bars.

STORING COOKIES

Cool cookies thoroughly before storing. Slide baked cookies onto wire cake racks with spatula. Do not overlap or stack cookies until cooled

Bars: Store in an airtight container or in the pan in which they are baked. cover the pan tightly with self-lid or aluminum foil.

Crisp Cookies: Store in a loosely covered container. If they absorb moisture from the air, crisp them in a slow oven at 300 degrees Fahrenheit for about 5 minutes. Cool.

Soft Cookies: Store in a tightly covered container. Slices of apple, orange, or bread placed in the container will help mellow and moisten the cookies. Change the fruit or bread often.

'Ono Lemon Coconut Bars

Makes 30

1-1/2 cups flour
1/2 cup confectioners' sugar
3/4 cup butter or margarine
4 eggs, slightly beaten
1-1/2 cups sugar
1 teaspoon baking powder
1/2 cup fresh lemon juice
3/4 cup coconut flakes

Combine flour with confectioners' sugar; cut in butter or margarine until crumbly then press onto bottom of 13 x 9-inch baking pan; bake at 350 degrees Fahrenheit for 15 minutes.

While crust is baking, combine eggs, sugar, baking powder, and lemon juice; mix well. Pour over baked crust; sprinkle with coconut flakes. Bake at 350 degrees Fahrenheit for 20 to 25 minutes.

PACKING FOR MAILING

Send only those types of cookies that can stand jostling. These include the rich moist bars and the cake-types (soft) drop cookies.

Mark your package: "PERISHABLE" and "HANDLE WITH CARE."

Macadamia and Cranberry Scones

Makes 12 scones

Indulge in some scones and tea, For a holi... ...ss free!

SCONES are like a biscuit, but different. Best served fresh, they are also good split and toasted the next day. They'll keep for up to two months, wrapped well and frozen.

Originally English, scones seem a lot like our biscuits. However, biscuits usually contain vegetable shortening or lard and milk or buttermilk rather than cream. Though some scone recipes call for milk, the classic cream scones contain rich sweet cream. Perhaps the biggest difference is eggs, which are a requisite for scones but absent from biscuit dough. In addition, while some bakers would faint at the suggestion of adding sugar to their biscuit dough, scones would not be what they are without it.

2-1/2 cups all-purpose flour
4-1/2 teaspoons baking powder
1 teaspoon salt
2/3 cup sugar
1/2 cup cold butter, cut into small pieces
1/2 cup finely chopped macadamia nuts
1/2 cup dried cranberries
1/2 cup heavy cream
3 eggs, in all
2 teaspoons milk

Lightly butter two baking sheets.

In a large bowl, sift together flour, baking powder, and salt. Stir in the sugar. Cut in butter until mixture resembles coarse meal. Stir in the nuts and cranberries. Make a well in the center. In a separate bowl, blend the cream with 2 eggs until smooth. Pour cream mixture into the well of the flour mixture. Stir until mixture holds together. Gather dough into a ball; it will be moist. Divide in half and flatten into discs on floured surface.

Turn dough out onto a lightly floured board and roll out to a 1-inch thickness. Cut out rounds using a 3-inch cookie cutter. Transfer to prepared baking sheets. Blend remaining egg and milk together and brush tops of scones with mixture. Bake at 350 degrees Fahrenheit for about 15 to 20 minutes, or until golden brown. Best when served hot with butter.

VARIATIONS

Macadamia Nut: Instead of cranberries, use (more) macadamia nuts.

Chocolate Chip: Replace cranberries with chocolate chip morsels.

Cranberry: Omit nuts; increase cranberries to 3/4 cup.

Cranberry Nut Bread

Makes 36 bars

2 cups sifted flour
1 cup sugar
1-1/2 teaspoons baking powder
1 teaspoon salt
1/4 cup shortening
3/4 cup orange juice
1 tablespoon orange zest
1 egg, beaten
1/2 cup chopped nuts
3/4 cup fresh cranberries, coarsely chopped

Sift together the first 4 ingredients. Cut in shortening until mixture resembles coarse cornmeal. Combine juice, orange zest, and beaten egg; pour all at once into dry ingredients; mix just enough to moisten. Fold in nuts and cranberries. Spoon into 9 x 5 x 3-inch loaf pan greased and lined with waxed paper. Bake at 350 degrees Fahrenheit for 1 hour until crust is golden brown. Cool completely before serving. This bread freezes well.

TIPS

Bake your favorite loaf of bread and place it on top of a bread board. Wrap in a clear, crisp wrap and tie at the top with a fashionable fabric bow.

Quick breads like muffins and biscuits are called so because they are quickly mixed and need no lengthy rising time before baking because they do not use yeast as an ingredient.

The general rule for baking quick breads, no matter what the shape, is to bake until a toothpick inserted in the center comes out clean

Pumpkin Bread

Makes 4 (1-pound) loaves

4 cups sugar
1 (29-ounce) can pumpkin
3 eggs, slightly beaten
1 cup oil
5 cups flour
1 tablespoon baking soda
2 teaspoons cinnamon
1-1/2 teaspoons cloves
1 teaspoon salt
2 cups dates (optional)
2 cups walnuts, toasted (optional)
Whipped cream cheese (optional)

Grease four 8 x 4-inch pans. Combine sugar, pumpkin, and eggs in a mixing bowl and beat until well blended. Add oil and continue to beat. Sift together flour, baking soda, cinnamon, cloves, and salt; add to pumpkin mixture and stir in dates and nuts. Fill prepared pans 3/4 full with batter. Bake at 350 degrees Fahrenheit for 1 hour, or until toothpick inserted in center comes out clean and bread has pulled away from the sides. Cool. Serve with whipped cream cheese. This bread freezes well.

MUNCHIES

Fudge

Makes about 1/2 pound

2 cups powdered sugar
1 (3-ounce) package cream cheese, softened
1/8 teaspoon vanilla
2 ounces unsweetened chocolate
1/2 cup nuts, chopped

Gradually stir sugar into cream cheese, add salt and vanilla. Melt chocolate in double boiler; cool slightly and stir into cheese mixture; add nuts and press into a well-greased shallow pan. Chill until firm and cut when set.

PERSONAL TOUCHES

Edible candy boxes made of chocolate

Unique or personalized ribbons to cinch bundles of tulle filled with candies for trims

Spray dried flowers with gold paint and tie them into the ribbon bow

Brown paper tied with raffia for that natural or Hawaiian look—tuck in sprigs of herbs

Use scraps of fabric, like yukata or kasuri, to make unusual ribbons

Squares of fabric make unique gift wraps—wrap and tie in "furoshiki" fashion

Dress up ordinary jars filled with homemade things with a round of colored paper or fabric covering the lid and tied with gold rope or twine

Chocolate and Macadamia Truffles

Makes about 24

14 ounces chocolate, chopped
1/2 cup heavy cream
1/2 cup macadamia nuts, lightly toasted and finely diced
1/4 cup sweetened flaked coconut, lightly toasted
Juice and finely minced zest of 2 limes
1 pound chocolate
2 cups sweetened flaked coconut, lightly toasted

Place 14 ounces of chocolate in a bowl. In a small saucepan, bring cream to a boil. Pour over chocolate and whisk until melted. Stir in macadamia nuts, 1/4 cup coconut, lime juice, and lime zest. Chill until firm.

Spoon chilled mixture into 24 balls of equal size. Roll in your palms to make smooth and round. Chill in refrigerator until firm.

Melt remaining 1 pound of chocolate over simmering water in the top of a double boiler. Dip chilled truffles into melted chocolate. Shake off excess chocolate and roll truffles in coconut; place on a plate and chill until firm. Repeat with all truffles. Truffles can be stored in freezer for up to 1 month.

TIPS

To melt dark chocolate, you don't have to chop it finely; however it's best to finely chop white and milk chocolate so that it melts quickly; if it gets too hot, it can scorch or become gritty.

Coconut Candy

Makes about 20 ounces

3 cups sugar
3/4 cup milk
3 cups fresh grated coconut
1/8 teaspoon salt
1 teaspoon white vinegar

Bring sugar and milk to rolling boil; add coconut and remaining ingredients. Cook until soft-ball stage. Remove from heat, add vanilla, and beat until ready to drop by teaspoonful on waxed paper. The secret to making good coconut candy is the amount of creaming. If you don't cream it enough, the candy will be soggy and sticky. The sugar will crystallize and the candy won't be creamy if beaten too much. Food coloring may be added to tint candy.

TIPS

To determine the correct temperature of cooked candy, insert a candy thermometer into the mixture, making sure mixture bubbles around bulb (do not rest bulb to rest against pan). Temperature will rise very rapidly once mixture reaches 220 degrees.

❖ Soft Ball Stage 234 to 240 degrees Fahrenheit
❖ Firm Ball Stage 242 to 248 degrees Fahrenheit
❖ Hard Ball Stage 250 to 268 degrees Fahrenheit
❖ Soft Crack Stage 270 to 290 degrees Fahrenheit
❖ Hard Crack Stage 300 to 310 degrees Fahrenheit

Sweet Party Mix

Makes 7 quarts

Nonstick cooking spray
1 (10-ounce) package Fritos corn chips
1 (6-ounce) package Bugles
1 (12-ounce) box Crispix
1/2 (10-ounce) package butter pretzels
1/2 (11-ounce) package Cheetos
1-1/2 cups butter
1 cup sugar
1 teaspoon garlic powder
1 tablespoon Worcestershire sauce

Preheat oven to 250 degrees Fahrenheit. Spray a large deep baking pan with nonstick cooking spray. Combine Fritos, Bugles, Crispix, pretzels, and Cheetos in prepared pan. In a saucepan, heat butter over low heat with sugar, garlic powder, and Worcestershire sauce; stir until sugar dissolves. Pour over cereal mixture; mix lightly. Bake uncovered at 250 degrees Fahrenheit for 1 hour, mixing lightly every 15 minutes. Cool and store in airtight containers.

Caramelized Macadamia Nuts

Makes 1 cup

1 cup macadamia nuts
3 tablespoons Hawaiian raw sugar
3 tablespoons water

To prepare caramelized macadamia nuts, heat water and sugar until sugar melts and turns color. Stir in nuts and cook, stirring constantly until water evaporates. Cool and store in clean jar with cover. Serve as a snack, condiment, or garnish on salads.

GIFT WRAPPING TIPS

Three to five single jars of jam or jelly in a box covered with pretty paper or foil, together with a little jam dish or spoon

A flask of liqueur with a suitable glass or jar of conserve

Add a suitable complementary item such as a wedge of cheese

A serving tray with a variety of preserves.

Use as containers for homemade food gifts: Strong box neatly covered with pretty wrapping paper or foil; baskets look good; new pan, colander, or serving tray

Use crumpled paper or polythene granules to keep glass and bottles safe

Tie a thin string or decorative tape or ribbon around a paper or cotton fabric topping

Use cheerful bold checked or plain fabric for pickles, chutneys, or sweet preserves, and very attractive patterns for conserves and curds

Cover jar tops with a circle of fabric or paper

Make attractive labels for jars. Clearly written labels are essential to identify products. Include name of product, date of preparation, expiration date and special notes.

Finish the gift with plenty of ribbons and an attractive card

Cinnamon-Sugar Spiced Macadamias

Makes about 2 cups

1/2 cup sugar
1-1/4 teaspoons cinnamon
1/4 teaspoon ground ginger
1/4 teaspoon salt
1 egg white
2 cups macadamia nuts

Lightly spray oil on baking sheet.

Stir the sugar, cinnamon, ginger, and salt together with a fork until blended. Whisk in the egg white until foamy. Stir in the nuts and spread mixture onto the prepared baking sheet. Bake at 300 degrees Fahrenheit for 10 minutes, stir, and bake an additional 10 minutes. Cool and store in an airtight container.

TIPS

Cinnamon is made from rolled, pressed, and dried tree bark, usually cassia (Cinnamomum cassia). It has a sweet flavor in both stick and ground form.

Microwave Mochi

Makes about 3 dozen pieces

1-1/2 cups mochiko (rice flour)
3/4 cup evaporated milk
3/4 cup water
1 cup sugar
1/2 teaspoon vanilla
Cornstarch or katakuriko (potato starch)
Few drops red or green food color, optional
Kinako (soybean flour), optional

Combine all ingredients except cornstarch or katakuriko in medium bowl; mix until smooth. Pour mixture into greased 5-cup microwavable tube pan. Microwave at medium high power for 10 minutes, rotating pan several times during cooking. Let stand a few minutes. Pull mochi from sides of pan; invert onto board dusted with cornstarch or katakuriko. Cool. Cut into 1/4-inch pieces using wet acrylic or plastic knife. Roll in kinako (soybean flour), if desired.

TIPS

To measure granulated sugar, dip nested measuring cup into sugar and level top of cup.

To measure liquid, use a liquid measuring cup placed on a flat surface. Pour ingredient into cup and check measuring line at eye level.

Spicy Kaki Mochi

Makes 5-1/2 quarts

Nonstick cooking spray
2 (12-ounce) boxes Crispix cereal
1/2 cup butter
1/2 cup light corn syrup
1/2 cup salad oil
1/2 cup sugar
3 tablespoons soy sauce
2 teaspoons hot pepper sauce
2 (1.05-ounce) packages Nori Goma furikake
3 (4-ounce) packages baby iso or small shoyu peanuts

Spray a large deep baking pan with nonstick cooking spray.
Place cereal in prepared pan. In a saucepan, heat butter with
corn syrup, salad oil, sugar, soy sauce, and hot pepper sauce;
stir over low heat until sugar dissolves. Pour over cereal;
mix lightly. Sprinkle furikake over mixture; mix lightly. Bake
at 250 degrees Fahrenheit, uncovered, for 1 hour, mixing
lightly every 15 minutes. Cool and stir in peanuts. Store in
airtight containers.

TIPS

Keep dry snack foods like chips and nuts stored in airtight
jars to preserve freshness.

Dry cereals in recipes may be substituted with your
favorite cereals—be creative!

To toast nuts, spread shelled nuts on ungreased baking
sheet. Watching closely and stirring frequently, toast in a
preheated 350 degree Fahrenheit oven 10–12 minutes or
until lightly browned.

Homemade Arare

Makes about 4 quarts

2/3 cup sugar
1/4 cup soy sauce
3 tablespoons water
8 drops hot pepper sauce
1 (15-ounce) box Rice Chex
1 package nori furikake
2 cups peanuts

Mix sugar, soy sauce, water, and hot sauce together; cook over low heat until sugar dissolves. Drizzle sugar mixture a little at a time over cereal and mix. Add furikake and peanuts; toss gently.

Spray two 9 x 13-inch pans with vegetable spray. Pour cereal mixture onto prepared pans and bake at 200 degrees Fahrenheit for about 1 hour; mix cereal every 10 to 15 minutes. Cool; store in airtight container.

TIPS

Most manufacturers and merchants agree that whole and ground spices have a two-year shelf life once opened. Best stored away from heat.

To measure brown sugar, pack into nested measuring cup and level top of cup. Sugar should hold its shape when removed from cup.

JAMS AND JELLIES

Guava Jam

Makes 8 (8-ounce) jars

8 large guavas
1 cup water
Sugar

Wash guavas; trim off blossom ends. Cut guavas into large cubes. Put 1/3 of the guava cubes and 1/3 cup of the water into a blender. Cover and blend at high speed until smooth, turning blender on and off when necessary to draw food down into the blades. Repeat until all of the guavas and water are blended; strain to remove seeds. Measure pulp into a large saucepan; add an equal amount of sugar. Cook over medium heat until mixture reaches jam consistency, about 30 minutes. Sterilize jars. Remove jam from heat. Pour into hot jars. Seal with melted paraffin while jam is hot.

PERSONALIZE GIFT JARS

Your imagination and creativity determines how your gift jars are "dressed." With colorful printed fabric, ribbon, and colored pens, you can quickly and inexpensively personalize your gift jars for that special someone.

Papaya Pineapple Marmalade

Makes 2-1/2 quarts

10 cups firm ripe papaya, chopped
1 cup fresh pineapple, chopped
1 cup orange juice
1 cup lemon juice
Zest of 1 orange
Zest of 1 lemon
2 tablespoons fresh ginger, grated
1/2 teaspoon salt
6-1/2 to 7 cups sugar

Combine papaya and pineapple in a large saucepan. Add juices, zest, ginger, and salt to the papaya and pineapple. Bring to a boil. Reduce the heat to low and continue cooking for 30 minutes. Add sugar and taste. Cook additional 30 minutes, stirring to avoid burning. Pour marmalade into hot sterilized jars and seal with paraffin. Keeps up to 6 months.

TIPS

Marmalade is a sweetened jelly made from citrus fruit and peel.

Poha Jam

Makes 2 cups

3 cups raw poha, husked and washed
1/4 cup water
1 cup sugar per each cup cooked poha
1 tablespoon lemon juice (optional)

Combine poha with water in a saucepan; cook slowly over medium heat for 30 minutes, stirring often, until there is enough liquid so the fruit won't burn. Remove from heat and let stand overnight or at least several hours.

Measure cooked poha; add equal amount of sugar and cool slowly over low heat, stirring constantly for 30 to 60 minutes. The jam is somewhat sticky and tends to stick to the bottom of the pot and burn, so when the juice thickens slightly or begins to sheet from the spoon, take it off the stove immediately and pour into hot, sterilized jars and seal with paraffin. Do not overcook the mixture as it tends to thicken as it sits.

TIPS

Jam is made of fruits or fruit juices, pectin, acid, and sugar. It is less firm than jelly and often some fruits are added to aid setting and enhance the flavor.

Quality jelly is clear and sparkling. It should retain its shape and quiver when removed from its jar.

GIFTS-IN-A-JAR MIXES

Amaretto Cocoa Mix

Makes 8 (pint) jars

10-1/2 cups nonfat dry milk
4 cups powdered sugar
2 (8-ounce) jars Amaretto flavored nondairy powdered
     creamer
3-1/4 cups chocolate mix for milk
2-3/4 cups nondairy powdered creamer
1/2 teaspoon salt

Combine all ingredients; mix well. Store in an airtight container. Decorate as desired and attach gift tags. Makes about 8 pint-size gift jars.

Include these instructions on your gift tag:
Combine 3 heaping tablespoons of Amaretto Cocoa Mix with hot water or milk. Top with whipped cream, if desired.

TIPS

You must have been intrigued by one of those adorable gifts-in-a-jar filled with nonperishable ingredients to make something scrumptious! Decorated with a square of brightly printed fabric and a colorful ribbon all you have to do is follow the simple instructions printed on the attached tag and you have a batch of home-cooked treats.

Today's busy lifestyle has created a major trend towards time-saving convenience foods, and mixes are the choice for many of our cooking needs. Mixes of all sorts have become an essential part of today's cooking and what better gift than a charming and practical gift-in-a-jar for you to make for your special friends.

Chocolate Chip Cookie Mix

Makes 36 bars

1-2/3 cups all purpose flour
3/4 teaspoon baking soda
1/2 cup sugar
1/2 cup brown sugar, packed
1-1/2 cups semisweet chocolate chips

Wash and dry thoroughly a 1-quart wide-mouth canning jar. Layer the ingredients in the jar as listed, pressing firmly with a spoon or mallet, after each addition. Make the layers as level as possible. Secure the lid and decorate as desired. Attach gift tag with instructions.

Include these instructions on your gift tag:
In a large bowl, cream 1/2 cup softened butter, 2 eggs, and 1 teaspoon vanilla extract. Add the contents of the jar; stir until well mixed. Drop the dough by heaping teaspoonfuls onto ungreased baking sheet, spacing cookies about 2-inches apart. Bake at 375 degrees Fahrenheit for 8 to 10 minutes, or until light brown. Cool and store in airtight container for up to 2 weeks. Makes about 2-1/2 dozen.

TIPS

Make lace lids by placing 7-inch doily over a painted lid or a circle of an interesting fabric

Brown paper bag or craft paper cut into a 7-inch circle and tied with twine or raffia makes the jars look very rustic

Coordinating fabrics cut into 7-inch circles or squares and placed one on top of the other can produce an interesting look

Cut squares or circles of fabric with fancy edge scissors

Cornbread Mix

Makes 1 loaf

1 cup yellow cornmeal
1 cup all-purpose flour
1/4 cup sugar
4 teaspoons baking powder
1/2 teaspoon salt

Sift together all ingredients and store in a plastic bag or air-tight container at room temperature. Makes 2-1/3 cups.

Include these instructions on your gift tag:
Pour Cornbread Mix into a bowl. Add 1 egg, 1 cup milk, and 1/3 cup melted butter or margarine; beat until smooth. Pour batter into greased 8 x 8 x 2-inch baking pan. Bake at 425 degrees Fahrenheit for 20 to 25 minutes or until knife inserted in center comes out clean. Makes 9 to 12 servings.

For muffins: Fill greased muffin tins 2/3 full with batter; bake for 15 to 20 minutes.

SALAD DRESSINGS AND SAUCES

Liliko'i Vinaigrette

Makes 4-1/2 cups

Juice and zest of half a lime
1 tablespoon sugar
1/2 teaspoon black pepper
1 clove garlic
1/2 teaspoon ginger, chopped
1 cup rice vinegar
1/4 cup liliko'i puree, unsweetened
3 cups salad oil
1/4 cup honey

Combine all ingredients in a food processor or blender and blend until smooth. Chill and serve over mesculun greens.

TIPS

Olive oil was first produced in the West by the Franciscan fathers, who brought olives to California in 1769.

Jazz up your veggies! Add crushed tarragon and fine bread crumbs to asparagus

Toss your salad greens with orange segments and orange marmalade.

Tomato Soup French Dressing

Makes about 3-1/2 cups

1 can tomato soup
1/2 cup sugar
3/4 cup vinegar
1/2 teaspoon pepper
1 teaspoon salt
2 teaspoons prepared mustard
1 tablespoon Worcestershire sauce
1-1/2 cups oil

Mix all in a bowl; beat well until smooth. Add oil slowly and continue beating until well blended. Store in covered jar in refrigerator. Serve over salad greens.

TIPS

Sauté chicory and escarole with garlic.

Grill or sauté endive and radicchio or add them to pastas and risottos.

Shred romaine lettuce to soups and stir-fries for a change.

The flavor and quality of any particular olive oil is determined by the variety of olive used, how it is cultivated, harvested, handled, and pressed.

Poppy Seed Dressing

Makes about 3 cups

1-1/2 cups sugar
2 teaspoons dry mustard
2 teaspoons salt
2/3 cup vinegar
3 tablespoons onion juice
2 cups salad oil
3 tablespoons poppy seeds

Mix sugar, mustard, salt, and pepper in a blender. Whirl until blended. Add onion juice and blend again. While blender is running, add oil slowly and continue mixing until thick. Add poppy seeds and whirl for a few seconds. Store in covered jar in refrigerator.

TIPS

Cilantro pairs well with garlic, lemon, lime, chiles, and onions and with other herbs like basil and mint.

Stir up a refreshing yogurt sauce with chopped cilantro, minced onion, salt and a dash of freshly ground black pepper. Serve with grilled vegetables or tossed greens.

For salads, look for the youngest and mildest leaves of argula. More mature argula is spicier but adds punch to salads.

Delicious Chocolate Sauce

Makes 2 cups

3 tablespoons butter
4 ounces unsweetened chocolate
2/3 cup evaporated milk
2 cups powdered sugar
1 teaspoon vanilla

Melt butter and chocolate over low heat in a heavy saucepan. Add milk and stir until blended. Add sugar and beat until smooth. Stir in vanilla. Store in covered sterilized jars. Refrigerate. Serve over ice cream, fruit, or angel food cake.

TIPS

Chocolate will keep for a year at room temperature. It is best to keep it stored below 70 degrees Fahrenheit.

Chocolate can sometimes be a little finicky, so for best results, store it in a cool, dry place, chop it even, and melt it gently.

Papaya Curry Marinade

Makes 1 cup

1 ripe papaya, peeled and seeded
3/4 cup orange juice
1/4 cup vegetable oil
2 tablespoons lemon juice
2 teaspoons curry powder
2 teaspoons salt

Place all ingredients in a blender or food processor and blend well. Store in covered jar in refrigerator. To use, spoon over poultry or pork and marinate overnight.

TIPS

Marinate meats in a zip-top plastic bag for even distribution of flavors and easy cleaning.

Marinate only in glass, stainless steel, or food-grade plastic so that the container will not react with the acid in the marinade.

Marinades, dry rubs, and pastes are easy ways to enhance the flavor of meat, poultry, fish, and vegetables.

Maui Barbecue Sauce

Makes about 5 cups

1 tablespoon butter
2 medium onions, diced
3 cups ketchup
1-1/2 cups chili sauce
1/2 cup cider vinegar
1/2 cup brown sugar, packed
1/3 cup molasses
2 teaspoons cayenne pepper
1/4 cup Worcestershire sauce
2 teaspoons liquid smoke
1/2 lemon
1/2 lime
1/2 orange
Salt and pepper to taste

Sauté onions in butter until translucent. Add remaining ingredients and cook about 30 minutes over medium heat until thick and still chunky. Use as basting sauce while grilling or broiling.

Zesty Cranberry Sauce

Makes 1 cup

1 (10-ounce) package fresh or frozen cranberries
3/4 cup water
1-1/2 cups sugar
4-1/2 tablespoons orange marmalade
Juice of 1 lemon
Juice of 1 lime

Rinse and drain cranberries. Boil water and sugar for 5 minutes. Add cranberries and cook without stirring until skins pop and cranberries are transparent, approximately 8 minutes. Remove from heat and stir in marmalade. Add lemon juice and lime juice and stir. Pour into serving dish, or pour into sterilized jars and seal. Refrigerate.

TIPS

Sealing jars: wash and dry jars, lids, and bands. Place jars on rack in large pot. Place lids in saucepan; cover jars and lids with water. Bring both pans to a boil; boil 10 minutes. Drain jars; fill to within 1/4 inch of tops. Wipe jar rims and threads. Quickly cover with lids and screw bands on tightly. Invert jars 5 minutes; turn upright. Sealed jars should be refrigerated unless sealed with melted paraffin.

CONDIMENTS

Raspberry Vinegar

Makes 5 (1/2-pint) portions

2 pounds raspberries
5 cups red or white wine vinegar
Sugar

In a large bowl, cover raspberries with vinegar. Cover with a
dish towel; let stand in a cool place for 4 days. Strain through a
jelly bag. Press fruit lightly; measure juice into a saucepan.
Measure 1/2 cup sugar for each 2-1/2 cups juice; stir to combine. Cook over low heat 15 minutes. Strain through a jelly
bag. Pour vinegar into washed and sterilized 1/2-pint jars or
bottles, leaving a 1/2-inch space from the top. Wipe rims of
jars or bottles with a clean damp cloth. Seal tightly with vine-
gar-proof lids.

Note: This recipe is best with fresh raspberries but can be substituted with frozen raspberries. However, fresh raspberries are
preferred since the texture is firmer.

TIPS

Toss a Wiki Wiki Middle Eastern Bread Salad by combin-
ing toasted pita bread pieces, diced tomato, cucumber,
sweet pepper, onion, and 2 tablespoons each of cilantro,
basil, and mint; season with olive oil and lemon juice
vinaigrette.

Mixed Herb Butter

Makes 1 cup

1 cup butter, softened
1/2 teaspoon each of minced fresh parsley, sage, oregano, and rosemary

Beat butter until creamy. Add herbs; beat again. Roll into cylinders; cover with plastic wrap and chill until firm.

TIPS

Combine 1/4 cup chopped cilantro, 1 teaspoon grated lemon zest, and dash of salt with 1/2 cup softened unsalted butter—delicious melted over hot-off-the grill chicken, steak, lamb, or fish.

Combine honey and butter when glazing cooked carrots.

Flavored butters may be served cold or at room temperature—use them as decorative garnishes or as instant sauces.

Garlic Oil

Makes 2 cups

5 cloves garlic
1 teaspoon black pepper
2 cups olive, peanut, or corn oil

Peel garlic cloves and place in clean bottle with cover. Add pepper and oil; seal. Allow to mellow 10 days before using. Will keep up to 2 weeks. Do not keep raw garlic stored in oil longer as it can spoil easily.

TIPS

Light oils infused with the flavors of herbs, spices, and fruits are a refreshing and healthful alternative to butter and other fats.

Use flavored oils for seasoning; they add depth of flavor and moisture to your foods.

Provençal Spice Mix

Makes 1-1/2 cups

Put this on any steak or chop bound for the skillet or grill.

Zest of 2 lemons
1/3 cup thinly sliced garlic
1/2 cup fresh rosemary leaves
1/4 cup fresh sage leaves
1/3 cup rock salt
1/4 cup freshly ground black pepper

Place lemon zest in food processor with the motor going; add remaining ingredients and process briefly until mixture has consistency of wet sand.

TIPS

To measure dry ingredients equaling less than 1/4 cup, dip measuring spoon into ingredient and level top of spoon.

To double a recipe, use twice the amount of each ingredient. If possible, salt, pepper and spices should not be doubled without tasting first.

Dried Herbs

Serves 4

Basil
Marjoram
Mint
Sage
Tarragon
Thyme

Divide fresh herbs into small bunches. Spread on baking sheets in thin layers. Bake in 120 to 150 degrees Fahrenheit oven for 45 minutes, or until dry and crisp. Remove from oven and cool; let stand for 12 hours. Remove stems; rub herbs lightly with hands to break up leaves. Store in airtight container in a cool dark place. Label as dried herbs can look alike. Use within 4 to 6 months.

TIPS

Dry rubs are compatible blends of dried herbs and spices that is rubbed on food before cooking. This method is frequently used to season foods for barbecuing.

Homemade mustards keep well in the refrigerator and mellow with time.

Spiced Seasoned Salt

Makes about 1-1/3 cups

1 cup salt
2 teaspoons sugar
2 teaspoons dry mustard
1 teaspoon dried oregano
1 teaspoon garlic powder
1 teaspoon curry powder
1 teaspoon onion powder
1/2 teaspoon celery seeds
1/4 teaspoon paprika
1/4 teaspoon ground thyme
1/8 teaspoon ground turmeric

Place all ingredients in a pint jar; cover and shake until mixture is completely blended.

TIPS

For something different, grind a clove of garlic and a handful of cilantro leaves in a mini food processor; stir in a few tablespoons of mayonnaise and a dash of hot sauce to make a Garlicky Green Mayonnaise. Great spread for a tomato or grilled chicken sandwich!

Pineapple Bell Pepper Relish

Makes about 1 cup

12 ounces pineapple, diced
1-1/4 ounces green bell pepper, diced
2-1/2 ounces red bell pepper, diced
1-1/4 ounces red onions, diced
Chopped cilantro to taste
Chopped scallions (green onions) to taste
1-1/2 ounces olive oil
1 teaspoon patis
Dash of lemon juice
Salt and pepper to taste

Combine all ingredients; mix well. Chill before serving.

TIPS

Preserving is one of the oldest and most satisfying forms of cooking. For centuries homemakers dried fruits, vegetables, and herbs; prepared pickles, chutneys, and sauces; and made jams and other scrumptious sweet preserves purely out of necessity. However, preserving is still a satisfying activity today that many people enjoy as a leisure pastime.

Today, there is a strong feeling for "old-fashioned" ways of years past and for the nostalgic delicacies that delighted our ancestors. While families obviously enjoy the results, cooks get great pleasure from offering these specialties as gifts, and presentation is almost as important as the preparation. These specialty gifts will certainly add a special touch to everyday meals and will also make welcome presents for all occasions.

Pickled Green Papaya

Makes about 2-1/2 cups

1 medium green papaya, pared
1/4 cup thinly sliced onion
1 small piece ginger root, minced
1 clove garlic, minced
2 Hawaiian red peppers, seeded and crushed
1/4 cup vinegar
1 teaspoon salt
1 teaspoon sugar
Dash of pepper

Cut papaya into halves and remove seeds. Grate papaya; add onion, ginger, garlic, and red pepper. Combine remaining ingredients and pour over papaya mixture; mix well. Refrigerate in covered container overnight before serving.

TIPS

Pickled fruits and vegetables and relishes are products with crisp, sour or sweet-sour flavor. Good quality vinegar is essential for pickling.

Finishing Touches

GIFTING IDEAS

Soup's On Fill a lovely soup terrine with soup mix, bread of your choice, and top off with a pretty ladle. Use fresh greenery or flowers for fillers.

Chocolate Delight Use a rectangular lauhala basket lined with a tapa print fabric and fill it with chocolate cookies, cookie mix, chocolate fudge, and a copy of your favorite food magazine or cookbook featuring chocolate desserts.

Coffee Break Place a package of cookies in a large mug along with a package of instant coffee or mocha mix; wrap with clear cellophane and top with a whimsical bow.

Tea for Two Take a nice basket or monkey pod bowl and center a teapot and 2 cups. Around them place tea mixes and dipped tea spoons for flavoring plain tea later. Don't forget to include some of your favorite tea snacks like a loaf of your favorite fruit bread and a lovely bow to brighten the basket.

A Touch of Class Take a bottle of flavored vinegar and place in a salad spinner along with a container of flavored oil. Add some salad condiments like croutons or even a set of salad servers and don't forget to include the recipes or a copy of this book. Even a 2-bottle wine container embellished with silk grapevines and filled with oil and vinegar would get raves.

77

Merry Christmas A white basket lined with red and filled with cookies, breads, jams, jellies, and everything delicious never fails to make the perfect gift. Let your creativity be your guide. Add miniature Christmas ornaments or stuffed animals to your basket. Top it with a huge, gorgeous bow made from a myriad of beautiful ribbons available at this time of the year.

Happy New Year Ring in the New Year with a festive basket for your party host. Fill a champagne bucket or an ice bucket (with handles) with an array of party time favorites. Tied to the handles and in the bucket place a nutmeg grater and whole nutmegs, a wine bottle opener, confetti, streamers, paper party hats, and noise makers.

TIE IT DOWN!
❖ ribbon, jute, cording, raffia
❖ varied widths of ribbons
❖ decorative wire garlands wrapped around
   the lid and twisted to secure

TAG IT!
❖ use colored pens to add zip
❖ draw or cut interesting designs to
   embellish tags

ADD UNIQUE TOUCHES
❖ attach bells, shells, or flowers to jar
   or tag
❖ tie recipe to jar
❖ attach wooden spoon, measuring
   spoons, or cookie cutters to jar
❖ wrap gift in dish towel

Portable Pie Prepared pastry dough wrapped in waxed paper, a rolling pin, a can of apple pie filling, or the ingredients for a fresh apple pie and pot holders all arranged attractively in a lovely ceramic or glass pie plate. Tie everything together with an attractive kitchen towel.

Sugared Fresh Flowers Crystallize fresh, edible flowers in sugar for use as garnish on a cake or cupcake. To make these attractive garnishes, cut stem close to the base of the flower. Dilute egg white with water; hold blossom with tweezers and brush egg white mixture on all surfaces of flower; sprinkle with superfine sugar. Place carefully on tray lined with waxed paper; set in warm, dry place 2 to 4 days, turning occasionally, until crisp. Will keep for months in a dry place. Suggested flowers: daisies, pansies, roses.

Pasta Basket Line a basket with red and white checkered dish towel, then fill with all the makings of a pasta dinner—spaghetti, fresh basil, garlic bread, tomatoes, mozzarella, and Parmesan cheese, flowers for the table, romaine lettuce, and a jar of Italian dressing. Wrap the basket in a clear, crisp wrap and tie with an attractive bow.

Scented Sugars Layer granulated sugar with aromatic, edible items like dried orange or lemon peel, vanilla beans, rose petals, or scented-geranium leaves. Let stand for a few days in tightly sealed jars to allow the infusion of scents into the sugar—adds a subtle flavor to coffee, fruit desserts, and baked items.

About the Author

MURIEL KAMADA MIURA is back with her time and taste tested advice for Hawai'i's cooks and food lovers. A graduate of the University of Hawai'i at Mānoa and Columbia University in New York, she is the author of seven cookbooks and an editor of four. Miura may probably be most recognized for her nationally televised cooking shows, *The New World of Cooking with Muriel* and *Cook Japanese* from the 1970s. Throughout her successful culinary career, Miura also has guest-starred on local cooking show *Hari's Kitchen*, judged food contests, taught community cooking classes and high school home economics, written articles about cuisine and food, and traveled as far as the New York World's Fair, where she participated as a featured demonstrator and won a prestigious award for outstanding demonstration in 1965.

Miura is comfortable with all types of ethnic cuisine but is known to add a touch of Hawai'i to her foods, reflecting the multiethnic flavors of Hawai'i's cultures. A Honolulu-born kama'āina, Miura lives with her husband Yoshio Kaminaka, and loves to sew and cook for her daughter, son-in-law, and grandchildren whenever they visit from the mainland. She is also active with numerous community service projects since her retirement from The Gas Company.